I LIKE SINGING SONGS

CORIN PENNINGTON

LEARNING CURVE MUSIC

ACKNOWLEDGEMENTS

This book wouldn't have been possible without all the wonderful support and encouragement from the children and staff of the schools, nurseries and children's centres I teach in. I would particularly like to thank the staff of Comet Nursery and Children's Centre for the guidance and support they have provided whilst I prepared this book. Thanks also to Globe Primary School, Mowlem Primary School, Sebright Nursery and Children's Centre and Thomas Fairchild Children's Centre for continuing to believe in the importance of music in children's lives. I need to thank all the children and their parents who have attended my classes over the years. I have learned so much from you all while teaching. I am especially indebted to the wonderful Sam Sweeney for all her time and advice, and to Michael Smee for his enthusiasm and encouragement. You really made the difference. However, my biggest thanks go to my Lily, Sophie, Lucas and Angie. Thank you so much for your patience and all the time you've allowed me to spend on the book. I love you guys.

CREDITS

Writing Credits:
I SEE A BOAT - Written by Angela Pennington. Copyright - Angela Pennington
KING OF KINGS - Written by Jimmy Cliff. Copyright - Beverleys Records Ltd
JAMBO - Written by Teddy K Harrison. Copyright - Santa Barbara Music Publishing
I'M A FREEBIRD - Written by Lily Pennington. Copyright - Lily Pennington
WHO LIVES IN THE JUNGLE - Written by Lucas Pennington. Copyright - Lucas Pennington

Recording Credits:
All instruments have been played and recorded by Corin Pennington
All songs arranged, produced and mixed by Corin Pennington for Learning Curve Music
Vocalist are Corin, Angela, Lily, Sophie and Lucas Pennington, Axel and Milan Bournas, Taylor MacKenzie, Riley Monaghan and Noah Moseley.

www.ilikesingingsongs.com

I LIKE SINGING SONGS

CONTENTS

MUSIC IS FUN

Every day that I teach music to children I have so much fun, that I find it hard to believe it's my "job". I wanted to share some of what I've learnt and observed on the way, and some of the songs that have given so much pleasure.

Music is fun, and teaching music to children is some of the best fun. As long as you enjoy what you're doing, the children will as well and what we learn with pleasure, we never forget.

The power of music is immeasurable, especially for the young. It builds personal and social skills, confidence and self-esteem and aids all areas of a child's development. Plus, for parents, it's a wonderful bonding experience to share with a child. Experts agree that speech, language, numeracy and memory all benefit from active participation in music. Exposure to music has even been proven to help sleeping and feeding patterns in babies.

You don't need to be able to play an instrument or be a musician to enjoy music - we all respond naturally to music, particularly children. Learning some new skills, while having a lot of fun, means you are growing with your child.

There are so many benefits to be had from incorporating sign language into music. Remember, young children can use their hands long before they master speech, so adding actions always helps them understand, remember and enjoy songs more.

Makaton Sign Language is embraced in most pre-school settings. With the signs and actions shown throughout this book you will be able to communicate better with your child, meaning greater understanding and less frustration. This liberating communication is a gift of freedom for both you and your child.

I believe that nothing is ever achieved without enthusiasm. As long as you are enthusiastic, have a good repertoire of songs and music and a few instruments, you will have a wonderful time making music with children. I hope this first collection of songs will become part of that repertoire and help you on your musical journey. Use the songs as starting points, adding your own words and stories. Why not improvise and let your child's imagination lead you?

We say that we "play" music. But we tend to forget that play is a serious matter! We now understand the importance of play in education - it gives children a chance to practise what they are learning. So let the music play and play with the music!

Playing with your children is one of the most powerful and valuable experiences that you will ever share. Children learn through imitation - give them something worth imitating.

We all want to help our children, and the role of parents in the educational journey cannot be underestimated. The academic value of music is unquestionable, but more importantly it feeds a part of your child that otherwise remains starved.

Passionate teaching is infectious and encourages everyone to get involved and try things out. Be that role model.

So sing to the children, let them sing to you, and don't forget,

MUSIC IS FUN

SHAKE 'EM UP HIGH

Shake 'em up high
Up in the sky
Shake 'em down low
Down by your toes

Shake 'em up high
Up in the sky
Shake 'em down low
Down by your toes

Everybody say
Hello (Hello)
Hello (Hello)
Hello (Hello)
It's nice to see you here
REPEAT

Hello Corin
Hello Corin
Hello Corin
It's nice to see you here

REPEAT, SINGING EACH CHILD'S NAME AND FINISHING WITH A VERSE FOR EVERYONE

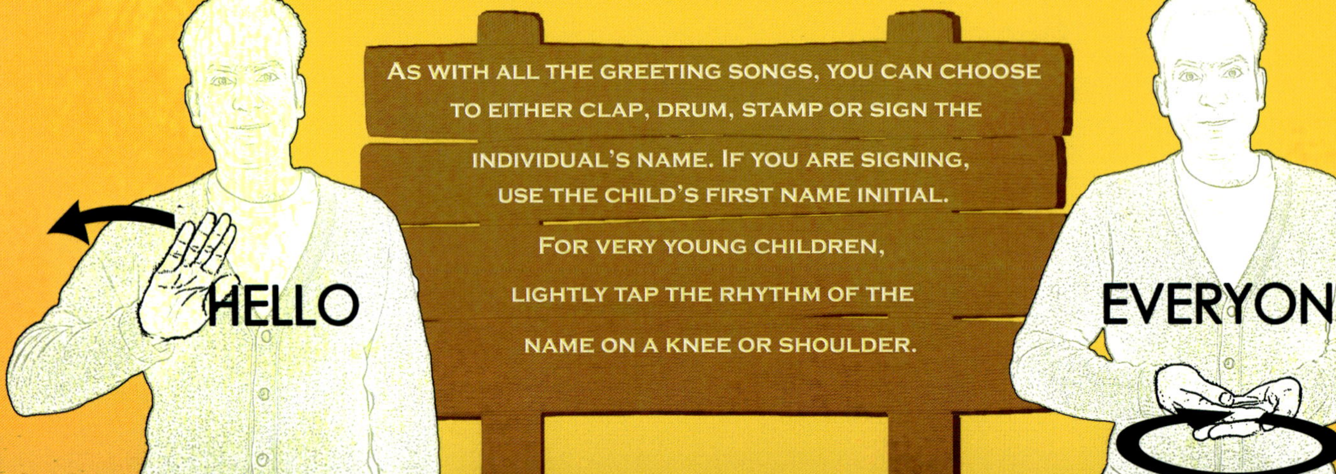

CO-ORDINATION GAMES

2

SHAKE AND STOP

Repeat this verse as many times as you like, add variations to the stop, such as roar, drum, clap, stamp. It's a good song to practise new sounds and actions. Any stop and start game is great for co-ordination and following instructions. I learnt this song from a book by Lynn Kleiner, an American music teacher, and it has been a simple staple of my classes ever since.

We're gonna shake and shake and shake and stop
Shake and shake and shake and stop
Shake and shake and shake and stop
Now we'll shake some more

THE BOO GAME

This is a really fun warm-up game, or just good fun at any time. Choose any piece of music you like, Northern Soul to House, Ska to Skiffle. Just let the music play and at random points stop the music. The aim of the game is to say "BOO" first, as soon as the music stops. As children get more used to the game you can add elements, like freezing or standing on one leg.

BIG FISH, SMALL FISH

Another great game,and you'll be surprised how well even very young children seem to get the joke. It always gets a laugh!
Get everyone to copy these two actions.
Say "Big Fish" and hold your hands close together.
Say "Small Fish" and hold your hands far apart.
The group leader should then start the game with a few "Big Fish" "Small Fish" commands. Everyone in the group should respond with the correct action. Then pass it around the circle, getting each child to say one command, with everyone in the group responding. It will take a few turns for everyone to pick it up, but I'm always surprised at how quickly children get it.

A FRIEND I KNOW

Lucas, Lucas, Lucas is a friend I know,
Everybody sing
Lucas, Lucas, who is next to you?

REPEAT, SINGING EACH CHILD'S NAME AND FINISHING WITH A VERSE FOR EVERYONE

THIS SONG IS EXCELLENT AS A WELCOME/ INTRODUCTION SONG.

EVERYONE SHOULD BE SAT IN A CIRCLE AND THE LEADER STARTS THE SONG.

THE QUESTION/ANSWER FORM WORKS VERY WELL TO GET THE WHOLE GROUP SINGING.

ONCE FAMILIAR WITH THE SONG THE GROUP CAN BE ENCOURAGED TO

ACCENTUATE THE SYLLABLES OF THE NAMES WITH CLAPS OR BEATS.

Hello Lucas, Hello Lucas, Hello Lucas,
It's nice to see you here.

REPEAT, SINGING EACH CHILD'S NAME AND FINISHING WITH A VERSE FOR EVERYONE

USE THE SIGN'S BELOW FOR THE LAST LINE

THIS SONG IS ANOTHER WELCOME/INTRODUCTION SONG. AGAIN SIT IN A CIRCLE AND THE LEADER STARTS THE SONG,

WAVING TO THE NAMED CHILD WHILST SINGING THEIR NAME, AND USING THE SIGNS BELOW.

NICE IS THUMB UP, DRAWN ACROSS THE CHIN.
SEE IS POINTING TO YOUR EYE.

YOU IS POINTING TO THE NAMED PERSON.
HERE IS POINTING TO THE GROUND.

AGAIN, ONCE FAMILIAR WITH THE SONG, ACCENTUATE THE SYLLABLES OF THE NAMES WITH CLAPS OR BEATS.

NICE SEE YOU HERE

I AM GREAT

I am great
I am the best
I'll always try
To help the rest

To always be
What they can be
That's the best of the best
From the morning 'til we rest

WHO I AM

Who I am
Is what I'll be
From now and evermore
I'll be myself
Pat my back
And let out one big

WHO LIVES IN THE JUNGLE?

7

Snakes live in the jungle,
Snakes live in the jungle,
Snakes live in the jungle,
What do the snakes say?

Fruit bats live in the jungle,
Fruit bats live in the jungle,
Fruit bats live in the jungle,
What do the fruit bats say?

Elephants live in the jungle,
Elephants live in the jungle,
Elephants live in the jungle,
What do the elephants say?

Orangutans live in the jungle,
Orangutans live in the jungle,
Orangutans live in the jungle,
What do orangutans say?

MY LITTLE BOY STARTED SINGING THIS ONE MORNING, LUCKILY I WAS LISTENING!

BEFORE STARTING THE SONG GET YOUR ANIMAL NOISES READY FOR THE END OF EACH VERSE.

TRY TO FOLLOW THE RHYTHM OF THE ANIMAL NOISES.

YOU'LL NOTICE EACH ANIMAL HAS AN EXTRA SYLLABLE/BEAT. WHO HAS FIVE SYLLABLES?

Beat chest and scratch armpits!

ORANGUTAN

LITTLE GREEN FROG

8

Mmm, Nnnnn
Went the little green frog one day
Mmm, Nnnnn
Went the little green frog
Mmm, Nnnnn
Went the little green frog one day
And they all went
Mmm, Nnnnn, bulululululu

SOUNDS AND ACTIONS

MMM IS CLOSED MOUTH

NNNNN IS TOUNGUE STUCK OUT

BULULULULU
IS WAGGLING YOUR TOUNGUE

But we know frogs go
(clap) la de da de da
(clap) la de da de da
(clap) la de da de da
We all know frogs go
(clap) la de da de da
They don't go
Mmm, Nnnnn, bulubububu

MR FROG JUMPED OUT

9

Mr Frog jumped out of his pond one day
And found himself in the rain
Said he
"I'll get wet, and I might catch a cold"

Aah

AAaah

AAAaaah

Choooooooo!

So he jumped in the pond again.

START THE SONG BY IMAGINING THE
MIDDLE OF THE CIRCLE IS A POND.
ALL JUMP INTO THE POND,
AND FOLLOW THE ACTIONS OF
THE SONG

BIG SNEEZES EQUAL BIG FUN !

KING OF KINGS

10

Lion says, I am king and I reign
Lion says, I am king in this range
No more kings must be in this backyard
Lion says, I am king and I reign.

Elephant says, I am king 'cause I'm strong
Giraffe says, I am king 'cause my neck is long
There's no doubt that they are all wrong
Lion says, I am king 'cause I'm double strong.

I'm king of kings, lord of lords in this land
No more bad hearts to any of you
'Cause I'm king
From the beginning, created king
Lion says, I am king and I reign.

THIS SONG WAS WRITTEN BY JIMMY CLIFF IN 1963,
BUT HAS BEEN COVERED BY MANY ARTISTS,
INCLUDING PRINCE BUSTER AND THE SKATALITES.
IT SEEMS THAT ALL CHILDREN LOVE THE SKA BEAT!

Show the lion's mane
LION
Clawed hands mime plodding
LION
Cupped hand shows shape of trunk
ELEPHANT
Hand moves up nec
then middle fingers close onto thumb
GIRAFFE

DO OUR EXERCISE

11

Gonna do our exercise
Gonna stretch and reach up high
Touch your head
Touch your toes
Touch your head
Touch your toes

Gonna do our exercise
Gonna stretch and reach up high
Touch your shoulders
Touch your knees
Touch your shoulders
Touch your knees

Gonna do our exercise
Gonna stretch and reach up high
Touch your head
Touch your shoulders
Touch your knees
Touch your toes

Gonna do our exercise
Gonna stretch and reach up high
Head, shoulders, knees and toes
Head, shoulders, knees and toes

Now BREAK

And BOUNCE

Gonna do our exercise
Gonna stretch and reach up high
Stamp your feet
Wiggle with your bottom and wiggle with the beat
Stamp your feet
Wiggle with your bottom and wiggle with the beat

Gonna do our exercise
Gonna stretch and reach up high
Stamp your feet
Wiggle with your bottom and wiggle with the beat
Stamp your feet
Wiggle with your bottom and wiggle with the beat

Gonna do our exercise
Gonna stretch and reach up high
Jump and clap and Jump and clap and
Jump and clap and Jump
Say it
Jump and clap and Jump and clap and
Jump and clap and Jump
Say it

Reach high, Reach high
Reach high, Reach high

AND BREATH ...

AND CROUCH

STAND UP ...

AND FREEZE

WAKE UP WAKE UP

12

Wake up, wake up
Everybody it's the morning
Get out of bed and stop your yawning
Get up, get up, you sleepy head
Time to get out of bed.

REPEAT

High, high, touch the sky
This is the song that you gotta try
Low, low, touch your toes
Start all again you know how it goes.

REPEAT

Wake up, wake up
Everybody it's the morning
Get out of bed and stop your yawning
Get up, get up, you sleepy head
Time to get out of bed.

REPEAT

High, high, touch the sky
This is the song that you gotta try
Low, low, touch your toes
Start all again you know how it goes.

REPEAT

JUMPING ALL

13

I can jump a song
I can jump it all day long
Jumping with my body I can
Jump it with the song
Jump, jump, jump, jump,
jump, jump, jump,
Jump, jump, jump, jump,
Jumping all day long.

I can stamp my feet
I can stamp them all day long
Stamping with my feet I can
Stamp them with the song
Stamp, stamp, stamp, stamp,
Stamp, stamp, stamp,
Stamp, stamp, stamp, stamp,
Stamping all day long.

I can clap my hands
I can clap them all day long
Clapping with my hands I can
Clap them with the song
Clap, clap, clap, clap,
Clap, clap, clap,
Clap, clap, clap, clap,
Clapping all day long.

I can wiggle my bottom
I can wiggle it all day long
Wiggling with my body I can
Wiggle it with the song
Wiggle it, wiggle it, wiggle it, wiggle it,
Wiggle it, wiggle it, wiggle it,
Wiggle it, wiggle it, wiggle it, wiggle it,
Wiggle it all day long.

DAY LONG

I can star jump
I can star jump all day long
Star jump with my body I can
Star jump with the song
Star, jump, star, jump,
Star, jump, star, you are a
Star, jump, star, jump,
Yes you are a star
Do a big dramatic yawn,
and everyone lie down to sleep.

I could go to sleep now
I could sleep the whole day long
Dreaming in my bed I can
Dream about the song then I can
Wake up
Jump up
Stamp up
Clap it up
Wiggle it up
Star jump up
Sing the whole day long

I can jump a song
I can jump it all day long
Jumping with my body I can
Jump it with the song
Jump, jump, jump, jump,
jump, jump, jump,
Jump, jump, jump, jump,
Jumping all day long.

Follow the actions of each verse for this song. You can also add any action the children think of.

I LIKE SINGING SONGS

14

I like singing songs
So I can singalong to
I like singing songs

I like singing songs
So I can singalong to
I like singing songs

I sing a song about a boat at sea
I sing a song about you and me
I sing a song about joining in
Find your favourite song and sing, sing, sing!

I like singing songs
So I can singalong to
I like singing songs

I like singing songs
So I can singalong to
I like singing songs

I sing a song about twinkle little star
I sing a song about a rusty old car
I sing a song about going to the moon
I sing a song about ZOOM ZO

I like singing songs
So I can singalong to
I like singing songs

I like singing songs
So I can singalong to
I like singing songs

I sing a song about ABC
I sing a song about 123
I sing a song about singing songs with me
So singalonga, singalonga, singalong with me!

Singalonga, singalonga, singalong with me
Singalonga, singalonga, singalong with me
Singalonga, singalonga, singalong with me
Singalonga, singalonga, singalong with me

I like singing songs
So I can singalong to
I like singing songs

I like singing songs
So I can singalong to
I like singing songs

OM ZOOM

I'M A FREE BIRD

15

I'm a free bird
Flying in the sky
Look how high
I can fly,

I'm a free bird
Fly with me
Fly with me
What can we see?

I'm a free bird
Flying in the sky
Look how high
I can fly,

I'm a free bird
Fly with me
Fly with me
What can we see?

Trees, trees
From up in the sky
Look so tiny
When you fly,

All the trees, trees
From up in the sky
Look so tiny
When you fly,

I'm a free bird
Flying in the sky
Look how high
I can fly,

I'm a free bird
Fly with me
Fly with me
What can we see?

Clouds, clouds
Up in the sky
They look massive
When you fly,

All the clouds, clouds
Up in the sky
They look massive
When you fly,

I'm a free bird
Flying in the sky
Look how high
I can fly,

I'm a free bird
Fly with me
Fly with me
What can we see?

People, people
From up in the sky
Look so tiny
When you fly,

All the people
From up in the sky
Look so tiny
When you fly,

I'm a free bird
Flying in the sky
Look how high
I can fly,

I'm a free bird
Fly with me
Fly with me
What can we see?

I'm a free bird
Flying in the sky
Look how high
I can fly,

I'm a free bird
Fly with me
Fly with me
What can we see?

I'm a free bird
Flying in the sky
Look how high
I can fly,

I'm a free bird
Fly with me
Fly with me
What can we see?

Aeroplanes, aeroplanes
Up in the sky
They look massive
When you fly,

All the aeroplanes
Up in the sky
They look massive
When you fly,,,

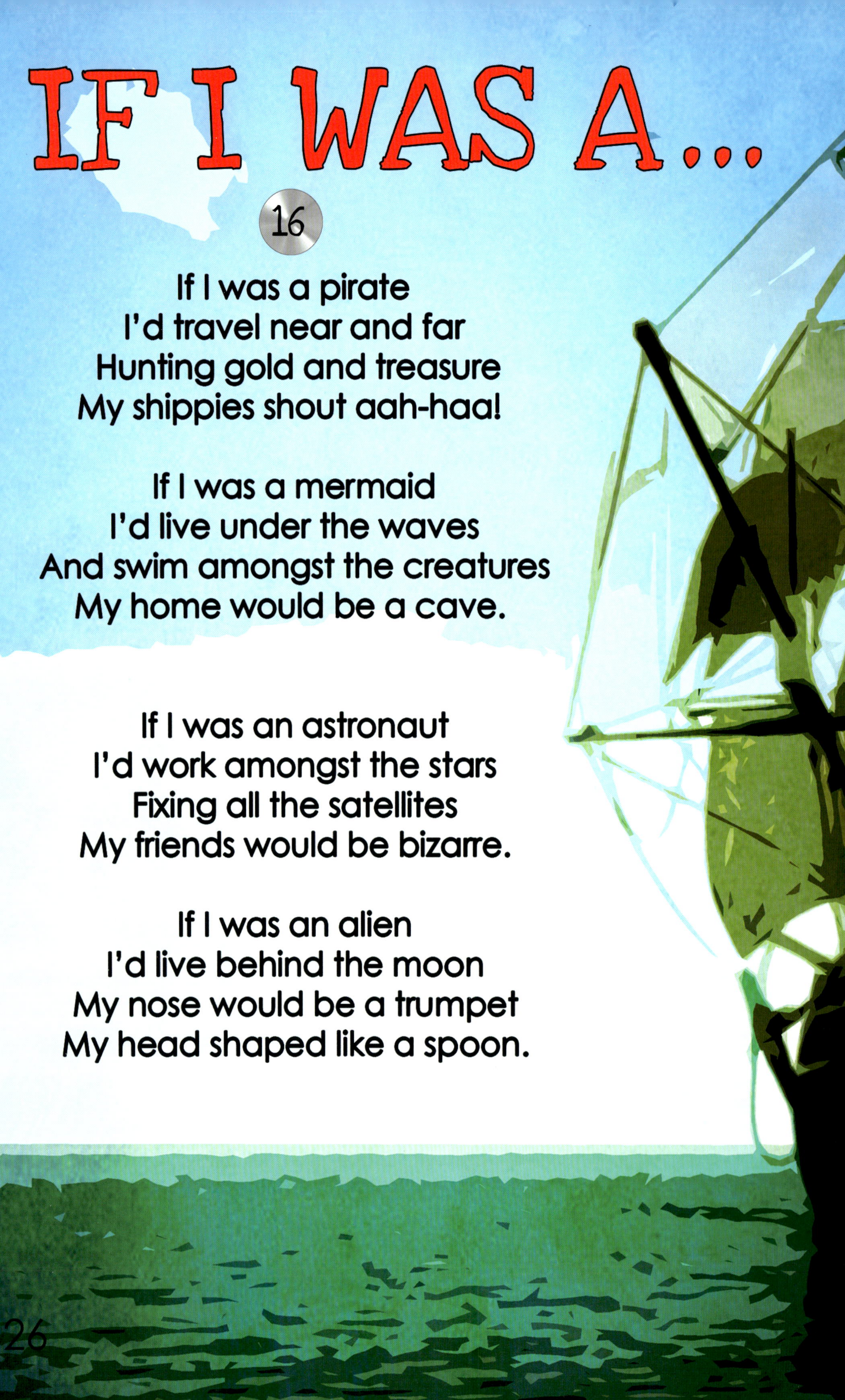

IF I WAS A...

16

If I was a pirate
I'd travel near and far
Hunting gold and treasure
My shippies shout aah-haa!

If I was a mermaid
I'd live under the waves
And swim amongst the creatures
My home would be a cave.

If I was an astronaut
I'd work amongst the stars
Fixing all the satellites
My friends would be bizarre.

If I was an alien
I'd live behind the moon
My nose would be a trumpet
My head shaped like a spoon.

If I was a pilot
I'd fly high in the sky
And navigate the aerospace
My crew right by my side.

If I was a firefighter
I'd slide right down the pole
Jump into my fire engine
Then I'd be on patrol.

If I was a dreamer
I'd dream a world for me
Full of love and happiness
Where everyone could be.

Happy and delighted
Satisfied and free
Living all together
Like the birds up in the trees.

I SEE A BOAT

I see a boat
Way out at sea
Where is it going
Is it coming for me?

Let's jump on board
And we will go
On an adventure
Row, row, row
Row, row, row
Row, row, row

On an adventure
We will go
Across the water
To a land I know

Jump up beside me
You will see
Adventures are waiting
For you and me
You and me
You, and, me

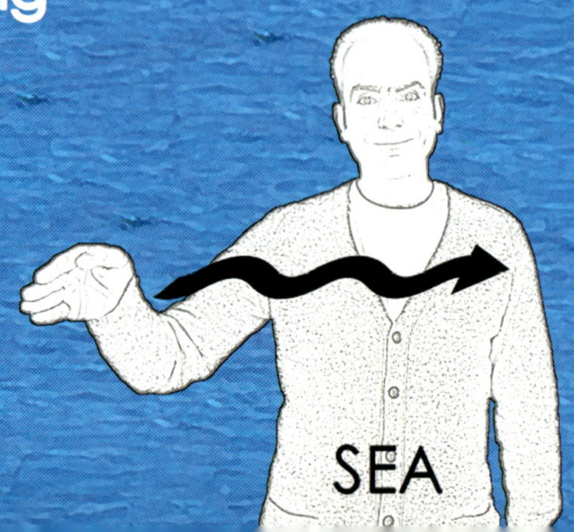

MAMA PAQUITA

18

Mama, Mama, Mama Paquita, Mama Paquita,
Mama Paquita buy your baby a papaya,
A nice papaya or a banana,
A nice banana for your baby to enjoy!
Mama, Mama, Mama Paquita, Mama Paquita,
Mama Paquita says "I haven't any money
To buy papayas or a banana,
Let's go to Carnival and dance the night away!"

Mama, Mama, Mama Paquita, Mama Paquita,
Mama Paquita buy your baby some pyjamas,
Some new pyjamas, a yellow blanket,
A yellow blanket for your baby to enjoy!
Mama, mama, Mama Paquita, Mama Paquita,
Mama Paquita says "I haven't any money
To buy pyjamas, or a yellow blanket,
Let's go to Carnival and dance the night away!"

This is an adaptation of a song "Mama yo quero", (I want my Mama) most famously sung by Carmen Miranda. I learned this version from the lovely people at Camden Music Services.

HEAR THE TRAIN

19

Hear the train riding over
Hear the train riding under
Over mountains, over hills
Through the valleys and the fields.

Shhhh shucka chucka chuck, hoo hoo!
Shhhh shucka chucka chuck, hoo hoo!
Shhhh shucka chucka chucka chuck,
Hoo hoo!

See the train roll across the bridge
Mountain side, ridge to ridge
Here it comes out the tunnel
See the lights and the funnel
Shhhh shucka chucka chuck, hoo hoo!
Shhhh shucka chucka chuck, hoo hoo!

And the sound of the train
As it's coming down the track
Is the sound that we love
'cos it's bringing people back,

Home again
Home again
Home again
Home again
Hoo hoo!

Hear the train riding over
Hear the train riding under
Over mountains, over hills
Through the valleys and the fields

Shhhh shucka chucka chuck
hoo hoo!
Shhhh shucka chucka chuck
hoo hoo!
Shhhh shucka chucka chucka
Chuck hoo hoo!

WHEELS ON THE BUS

The wheels on the bus go round and round,
round and round, round and round,
The wheels on the bus go round and round,
All day long

The horn on the bus goes beep beep beep,
beep beep beep, beep beep beep,
The horn on the bus goes beep beep beep,
All day long

The wipers on the bus go swish swish swish,
swish swish swish, swish swish swish,
The wipers on the bus go swish swish swish,
All day long

The doors on the bus go open and shut,
open and shut, open and shut,
The doors on the bus go open and shut,
All day long

The people on the bus go up and down,
up and down, up and down,
The people on the bus go up and down,
All day long

RIGHT, LET'S GET OUR BAND TOGETHER!

The shakers on the bus go shake shake shake,
shake shake shake, shake shake shake,
The shakers on the bus go shake shake shake,
All day long

The drums on the bus go boom boom clap,
boom boom clap, boom boom clap,
The drums on the bus go boom boom clap,
All day long

The band on the bus makes lots of noise,
lots of noise, lots of noise,,
The band on the bus makes lots of noise,
All day long

STEAM TRAIN

21

I'm a steam train a-rolling,
Down the track,
Over the rails I go clickety-clack
Hurry, hurry, hurry!
To my destination
Cos the passengers are waiting
At the next station!

WOOH WOOH!
WOOH WOOH!

The fireman on the footstep putting coal on the fire,
The steam pressure's rising
Higher and higher
Chuff, chuff, chuff!
Will I make it up that hill?
Hoo hoo goes my whistle
Yes of course I will!

WOOH WOOH!
WOOH WOOH!

I'm a steam train a-rolling,
Down the track,
Over the rails I go clickety-clack
Hurry, hurry, hurry!
To my destination
Cos the passengers are waiting
At the next station!

WOOH WOOH!
WOOH WOOH!
WOOH WOOH!
WOOOOOH

SPRING SONGS

YOU ARE THE SEASONS

You are the springtime,
The lovely springtime,
You make the flowers start to grow.
You wake the world up,
A new beginning
A time to say everybody hello.

Try and learn each of these seasonal variations of "You Are My Sunshine". This is the 2nd verse on track

22

SPRING FLOWERS

Sung to "Twinkle Twinkle"
How many spring flowers can you think of?

Crocuses and Daffodils
Growing on the sunny hills
Cherry blossom on the tree
Snowdrops, Tulips, you will see
Poppies, Pansies, Bluebells grow
The sun is coming back you know

THE PITTER-PATTER RAIN CHANT

Pitter-patter, pitter-patter,
The rain goes on for hours
And though it keeps me in the house
It's very good for flowers!

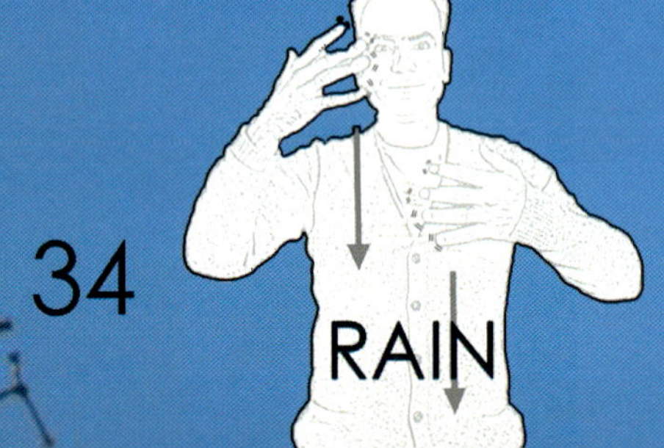

SUMMER SONGS

YOU ARE THE SEASONS

You are the summer
The only summer
You make me happy, when skies are blue
You shine your sunlight
Down upon me
And it makes me feel brand new.

Try and learn each of these seasonal variations of "You Are My Sunshine". This is the 3rd verse on track

22

HELLO MR SUN

Hello Mr Sun hello hello
Hello Mr Sun hello
Shine down shine down
And make my flowers grow.

SUN, SUN YOU ARE BRIGHT

Sung to "Row, Row, Row your boat"

Sun, Sun you are bright
Shine your light on me
If it is a hot day
I'll put a hat on me.

Sun, Sun you are bright
Make a rainbow for me
If you're shining while it's raining
That is what we see.

Sun, Sun where have you gone
Are you in the clouds?
Will you come back now
If I sing really loud?

SUN

RAINBOW

AUTUMN SONGS

YOU ARE THE SEASONS

Now it's the Autumn
The misty Autumn
And all the leaves are on the ground,
The nights are longer
It's getting colder
I think that winter is coming around.

Try and learn each of these seasonal variations of "You Are My Sunshine". This is the 4th verse on track

22

AUTUMN TIME IS HERE

Sung to "Twinkle Twinkle"

Autumn, Autumn time is here,
Soon the leaves will disappear
Misty mornings, starry nights
The days are short, turn on the lights
Autumn, Autumn time is here,
Soon the leaves will disappear.

AUTUMN LEAVES

Sung to 'London Bridge is falling down"

Autumn leaves are falling down,
Falling down, falling down,
Autumn leaves are falling down,
Red, orange yellow and brown.

BONFIRE NIGHT

Sung to "Hot cross buns"

Bonfire night, Bonfire night
Fireworks and sparklers
On bonfire night
Warm yourself up, with a great big hug
Gather round the fire with some soup in your mug.

FIREWORKS

WINTER SONGS

YOU ARE THE SEASONS

You are my snowflake,
My coldest snowflake,
You make me happy when you fall.
You'll never know dear,
How much I love you,
When I roll you into a snowball.

Try and learn each of these seasonal variations of "You Are My Sunshine". This is the 5th verse on track

22

ICY FINGERS, ICY TOES

Sung to "Twinkle Twinkle"

Icy fingers, icy toes,
Bright red cheeks and bright red nose.
Watch the snowflakes as they fall,
Try so hard to count them all.
Build a snowman way up high,
See if he can touch the sky.

SNOW IS FALLING

Sung to "Freres Jacques"

Snow is falling *(repeat)*
On the ground *(repeat)*
Scrunch it into snowballs *(repeat)*
Throw them around *(repeat)*

INCY WINCY WINTER

Incy Wincy spider climbed into a tree,
Down came the snow and made poor Incy freeze,
Out came the sun and melted all the snow,
Then Incy Wincy Spider had another go.

SNOW

23

Jambo
Jambo bwana
Habari gani?
Mzuri sana
Wageni mwakaribishwa
Kenya yetu
Hakuna matata

Original

THIS IS A VERY WELL-KNOWN
KENYAN POP SONG
FROM 1982 BY
THEM MUSHROOMS

BWANA

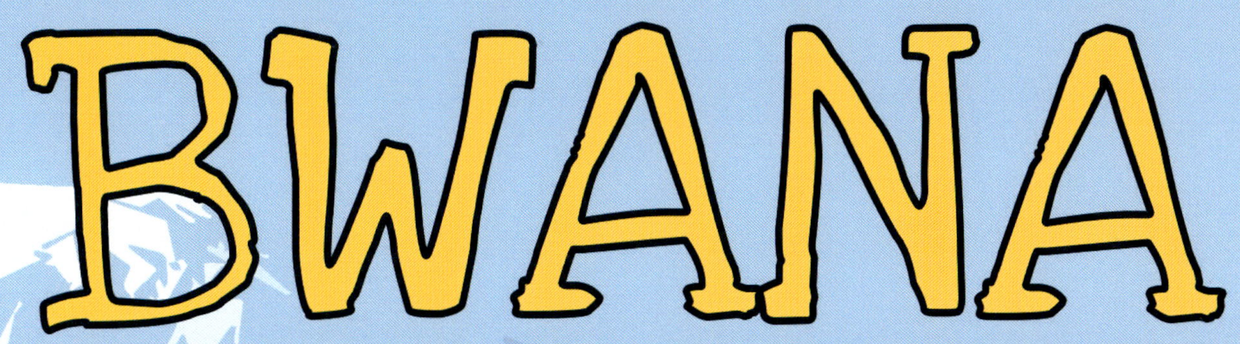

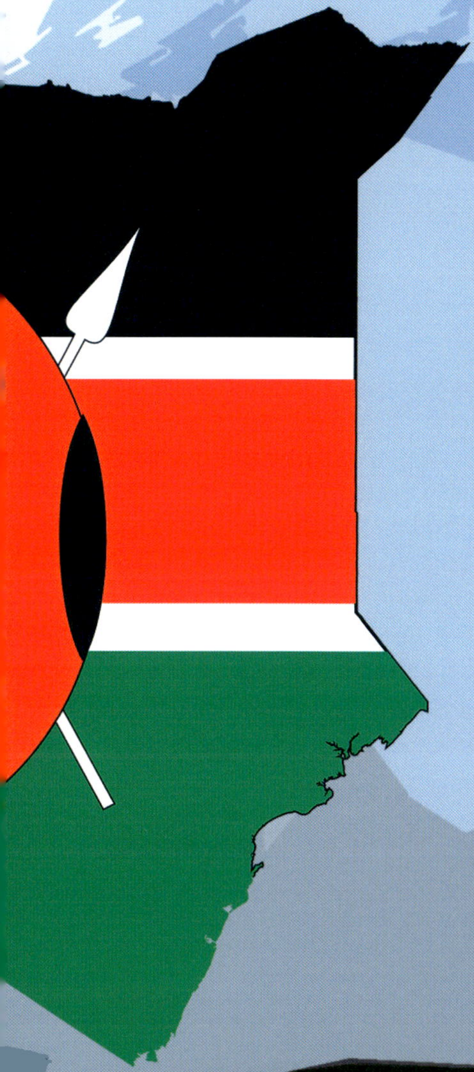

Hello
Hello Mister
How are you?
Very fine
Visitors are welcome
Our (country) Kenya
(there are) no worries

Translation

UP ABOVE MY HEAD

24

Up above my head *(up above my head)*
I hear music in the air *(I hear music in the air)*
Up above my head *(up above my head)*
I hear music in the air *(I hear music in the air)*
Up above my head *(up above my head)*
I hear music in the air *(I hear music in the air)*
Yes I do believe, yes I do believe
There is music in the air

Up above my head *(up above my head)*
I hear trumpets in the air *(I hear trumpets in the air)*
Up above my head *(up above my head)*
I hear trumpets in the air *(I hear trumpets in the air)*
Up above my head *(up above my head)*
I hear trumpets in the air *(I hear trumpets in the air)*
Yes I do believe, yes I do believe
There are trumpets in the air

Sister Rosetta Tharpe

Up above my head *(up above my head)*
sunny skies are in the air *(sunny skies are in the air)*
Up above my head *(up above my head)*
sunny skies are in the air *(sunny skies are in the air)*
Up above my head *(up above my head)*
sunny skies are in the air *(sunny skies are in the air)*
Yes I do believe, yes I do believe
sunny skies are in the air

Up above my head *(up above my head)*
helicopters in the air *(helicopters in the air)*
Up above my head *(up above my head)*
helicopters in the air *(helicopters in the air)*
Up above my head *(up above my head)*
helicopters in the air *(helicopters in the air)*
Yes I do believe, yes I do believe
There's helicopters in the air

OOH!!!

"UP ABOVE MY HEAD" IS A GOSPEL SONG.
ORIGINALLY RECORDED IN THE 1940S BY PIONEERING GOSPEL SINGER'S SISTER ROSETTA THARPE AND MARIE KNIGHT .
I WAS INTRODUCED TO THE SONG VIA DAN ZANES "FAMILY MUSIC WORKSHOP".
I'VE ADAPTED THE LYRICS, NO DISRESPECT MEANT, AND MADE IT NON RELIGIOUS.
THIS IS ANOTHER SONG THAT IS GREAT FOR IMPROVISING WITH.

BAA BAA BLACK SHEEP

25

Baa baa black sheep have you any wool?
C C G G A B C-A G
Yes sir yes sir three bags full
F F E E D D C
One for the master
G G G F F
One for the dame
E E E D
And one for the little boy
D G G G F-G A
who lives down the lane.
F E D D C

Thank you said the master
C C C E G G
Thank you said the dame
A B C A G
Thank you said the little boy
F F F F E-E E
Who lives down the lane.
E D D D C

TWINKLE TWINKLE

26

Twinkle twinkle little star
C-C G-G A-A G
How I wonder what you are
F F E-E D D C
Up above the world so high
G G F F E E D
Like a diamond in the sky
G G F F E E D
Twinkle twinkle little star
C-C G-G A-A G
How I wonder what you are.
F F E-E D D C

ANYONE WITH CHILDREN WILL KNOW THESE WORDS!
WHAT IS NEEDED IS A WAY TO KEEP THEM INTERESTING FOR EVERYONE.
YOU CAN LEARN HOW TO SIGN THE SONGS WITH THE CHILDREN.
YOU COULD ALSO LEARN HOW TO PLAY THE MELODIES ON A XYLOPHONE.
THE LETTERS UNDERNEATH EACH WORD, ARE THE MUSICAL NOTES.
USE THE SIMPLE XYLOPHONE SIGN BELOW TO HELP YOU.
ONCE YOU GIVE IT A GO YOU WILL BE AMAZED AT HOW MANY TUNES
YOU WILL BE ABLE TO WORK OUT.

WHY NOT TRY THE
"TWINKLE TWINKLE CHALLENGE"
USING THE MELODY TO MAKE UP SONGS.

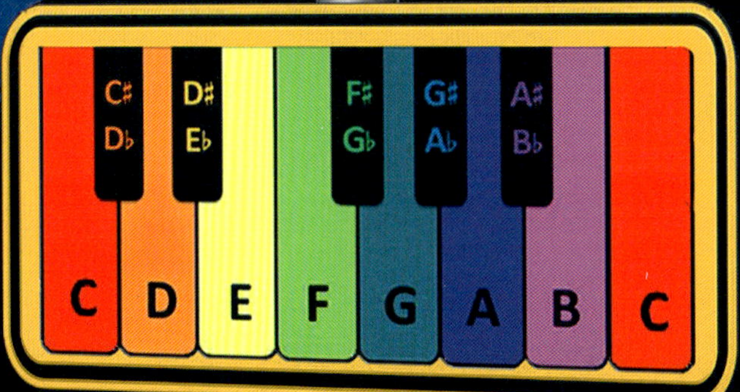

OLD MACDONALD

27

Old MacDonald had a farm, E-I-E-I-O
And on that farm he had some sheep, E-I-E-I-O
With a baa-baa here, and a baa-baa there
Here a baa, there a baa, everywhere a baa-baa
Old MacDonald had a farm, E-I-E-I-O

Old MacDonald had a farm, E-I-E-I-O
And on that farm he had some cows, E-I-E-I-O
With a moo-moo here, and a moo-moo there
Here a moo, there a moo, everywhere a moo-moo
Old MacDonald had a farm, E-I-E-I-O

Old MacDonald had a farm, E-I-E-I-O
And on that farm he had some ducks, E-I-E-I-O
with a quack-quack here, and a quack-quack there
Here a quack, there a quack, everywhere a quack-quack
Old MacDonald had a farm, E-I-E-I-O

ROW ROW

28

Row row row your boat, gently down the stream,
Merrily, merrily, merrily, merrily, life is but a dream

Row row row your boat, gently down the stream,
If you see a Crocodile, don't forget to scream

Row row row your boat, gently to the shore,
If you see a Lion, don't forget to roar

Row row row your boat, gently down the river,
If you see a Polar Bear, don't forget to shiver

Row row row your boat, all across the sea,
If you see me passing by, wave your hand at me

Row row row your boat, all across the puddle,
If you see your teddy bear, give him a great big cuddle

Row row row your boat, all around the bath,
If you see a tiny turtle, don't forget to laugh

Row row row your boat, all around the loo,
Don't forget to flush it if you do a ...!!!

Row row row your boat, gently down the stream,
Merrily, merrily, merrily, merrily, life is but a dream

CLAPPING AND

I LOVE THE SIMPLE, INSTANT FUN OF CLAPPING AND CHANTING SONGS
THE LEADER SAYS EACH PHRASE, THE GROUP COPIES.

LEMONADE, CRUNCHY ICE 29

A fantastic starter. I've included the response in this one to make it clear. Let people try being the "lemonade leader".

Lemonade *Lemonade*
Crunchy ice *Crunchy ice*
Beat it once *Beat it once*
Beat it twice *Beat it twice*
Turn around *Turn around*
Touch the ground *Touch the ground*
FREEZE *FREEZE*

I LIKE BANANAS, COCONUTS AND GRAPES

30

I like bananas, coconuts and grapes
I like bananas, coconuts and grapes
I like uhh *(flex right bicep)* **and coconuts and grapes**
I like uhh *(flex right bicep)* **and uhh** *(flex left bicep)* **and grapes**
I like uhh *(flex right bicep)* **and uhh** *(flex left bicep)* **and URRRR**
That's why they call me TARZAN OF THE APES!

HERE'S MY RHYTHM, NOW HERE'S MY BEAT

Clapping games are a progression from the chanting songs. The leader starts, and the group claps in response. Again, repeat each phrase and action.

31

Here's my rhythm, now here's my beat
Leader claps a rhythm. Start simply and get more complex.
We got your rhythm, now here's your beat
Group copies the rhythm. Repeat each pattern twice.

CHANTING SONGS

THEY WORK, EVEN IF THE GROUP DOESN'T KNOW THE WORDS! TRY WITH VARIATIONS OF DELIVERY, LOUD, QUIET, FAST,SLOW.

FLEA, FLY, MOSQUITO 32

This is a great, high energy vocal warm-up. No claps needed. Act out the itchy itchy and finish with a big spray can gesture.

Flea,
Flea, fly,
Flea, fly, mosquito
Oh no, no, no more mosquito
Itchy itchy scratchy scratchy, ooh I got one down my backy
Beat that big bug with the bug spray
SSSHHHHHHHHH

BOOM CHICKA-BOOM 33

Again the leader says each phrase, and the group repeats.

Boom chicka-boom
Boom chicka-boom, boom
Boom chicka chicka chicka chicka chicka-boom
OK
UH HUH
ALRIGHT
ONE MORE TIME

Boom chicka-boom
Boom chicka-boom boom
Boom chicka racka chicka racka chicka-boom
OK
UH HUH
ALRIGHT
ONE MORE TIME

SONGS AND GAMES

One of my favourite props is a large children's play parachute. Colourful, fun and irresistible, they can be bought very cheaply. Children love playing with and under them. There are loads of songs that work brilliantly with the parachute. It really encourages group work, co-ordination, and it's lots of fun. Using the parachute is always a great way to end a session. A great starting point is to play some hiding games, as that's all children will want to do at first anyway!

Everyone sits in a circle, and holds the parachute up to their eyes. On "Boo", everyone pulls down the parachute, and shouts "BOO" There's lots of room for variations too.

PEEK A BOO 34

Peek a boo
Where are you
Hiding in your place?
Peek a boo
I see you
With your smiling face.

You need to take some care, but this is good for letting all or some of the children in a group hide and be found.

(sung to Freres Jaques tune)

Where are the children?
Where are the children?
There they are
There they are
Put them all away now
Put them all away now
Where have they gone?
Where have they gone?

Try any song with a POP in it.
Here are a couple I've discovered.

FOR PARACHUTES

THREE BIG BALLOONS 35

Three big balloons, yellow, green and blue
One went pop, and then there were two.

Two big balloons, ready for some fun
One went pop, and then there was one.

One big balloon, playing in the sun
It went pop, and then there were none.

POPCORN 36

For this song, everyone stands in a circle holding the parachute. Mime the actions and sounds, it's all about the dynamics!

Put in the popcorn (chu, chu, chu)
Put in the salt (shucka, shucka, shucka)
Pour in the oil (glug, glug, glug)
Turn on the heat (Shhhhhhhhhh)
Sizzle, sizzle, sizzle, sizzle,
sizzle, sizzle, sizzle, sizzle,
sizzle, sizzle, sizzle, sizzle,
POP!

Here are a few of the songs I find work well with the parachute.

1, 2, 3, 4, 5 Once I Caught A Fish Alive - *good responding and turn taking game. Use a toy fish as a prop.*

5 Little Monkeys - *use toy monkeys, teddies, frogs and vary lyrics.*

Row, Row, Row Your Boat - *all sit in a circle and work together.*

Finally, a song for co-ordinating group movement. With older children stand and move, babies love it when you're sitting.

Round and round and round and round and UP UP UP
ound and round and round and round and DOWN DOWN DOWN
Round and round and round and round and IN IN IN
Round and round and round and round and OUT OUT OUT.

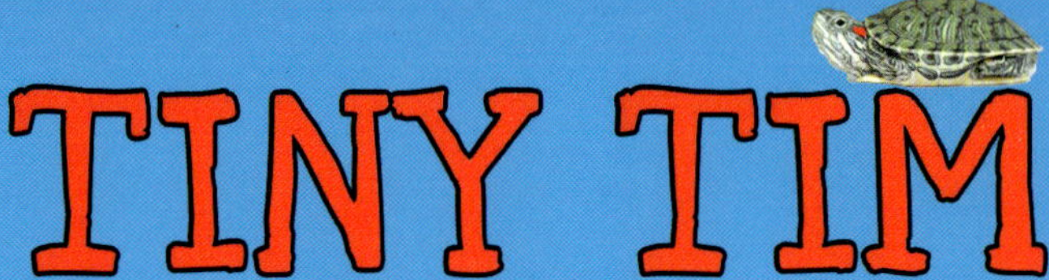

I had a little turtle
His name was Tiny Tim
I put him in the bathtub
To see if he could swim

He drank up all the water
And ate up all the soap
And now he's in his bed
He's got a bubble in his throat

Bubble

Bubble

Bubble

POP!

TURTLE BATH WATER SOAP

OPEN SHUT THEM

Open shut them, open shut them,
Give a little clap,

Open shut them, open shut them
Put them in your lap.

Creep them creep them
Creep them creep them
Right up to your chin,

Open up your little mouth
But do not put them in.

Wave them, wave them,
Wave them, wave them
Wave them way up high,

Wave your hands
To all your friends
That's how we say goodbye.

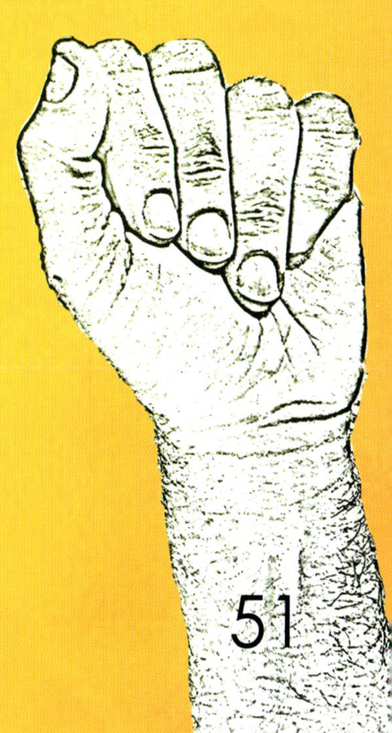

YOU HEAR THIS SONG IN MANY NURSERIES AND PLAYGROUPS, WITH LOTS OF VARIATIONS. TRY IT AS A GOODBYE SONG.

A
B
C
G
H
I
M
N
O
S
T
U
Y
Z

SIGNING ALPHABET

Learning the signing alphabet is easier than you think. Start by learning the vowels. Many of the letters are also words, 2 taps of M is Mummy, 2 taps of F is Daddy. To sign someone's name, you use their first initial. Animals are also fun first signs. Teaching young children to use sign language encourages speech and language development, and can be a very useful pre-speech communication system.

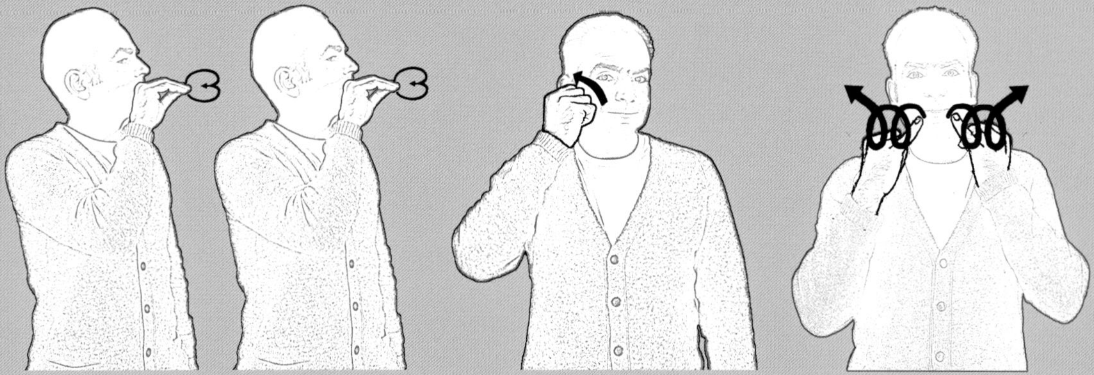

Baa Baa black sheep

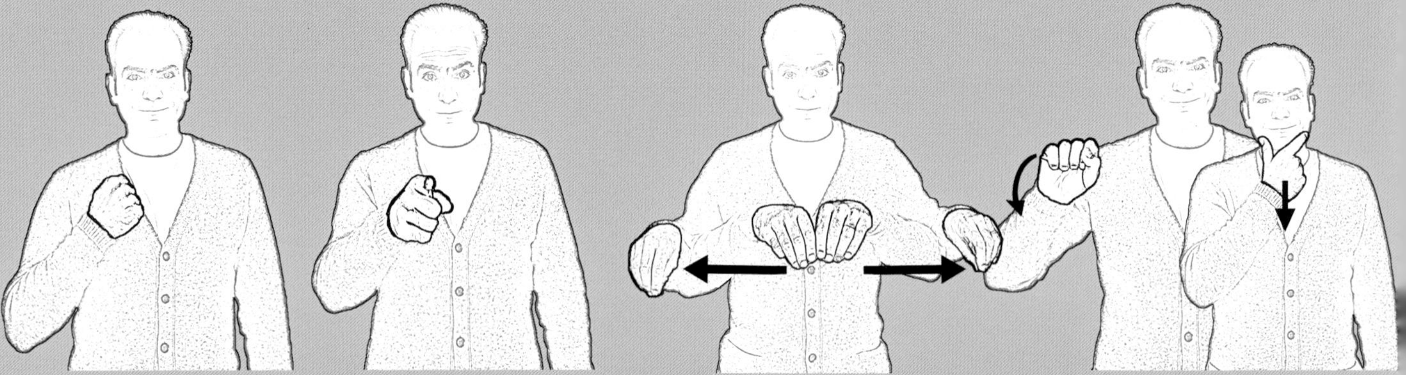

Have you *any* wool Yes sir

Three bags full *Master* Dame

Little boy *who* lives *down the* lane

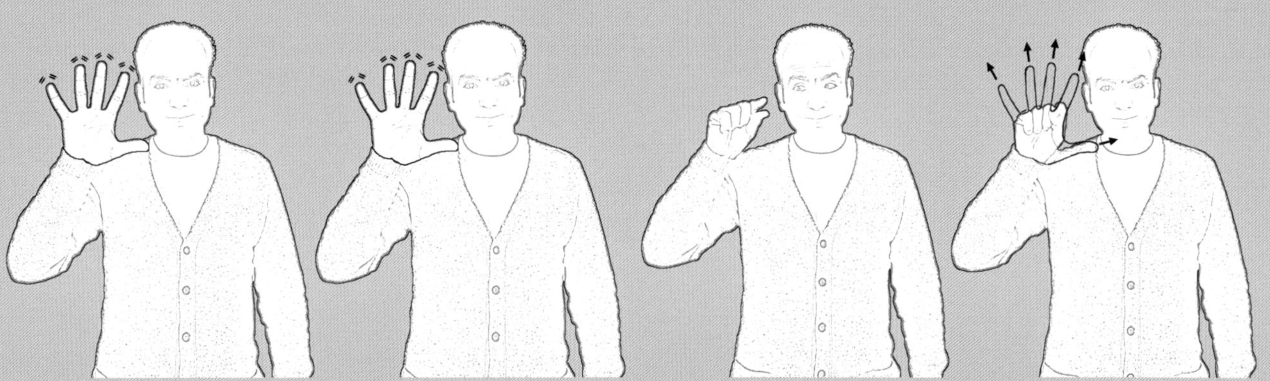

Twinkle twinkle little star

How I wonder what you *are*

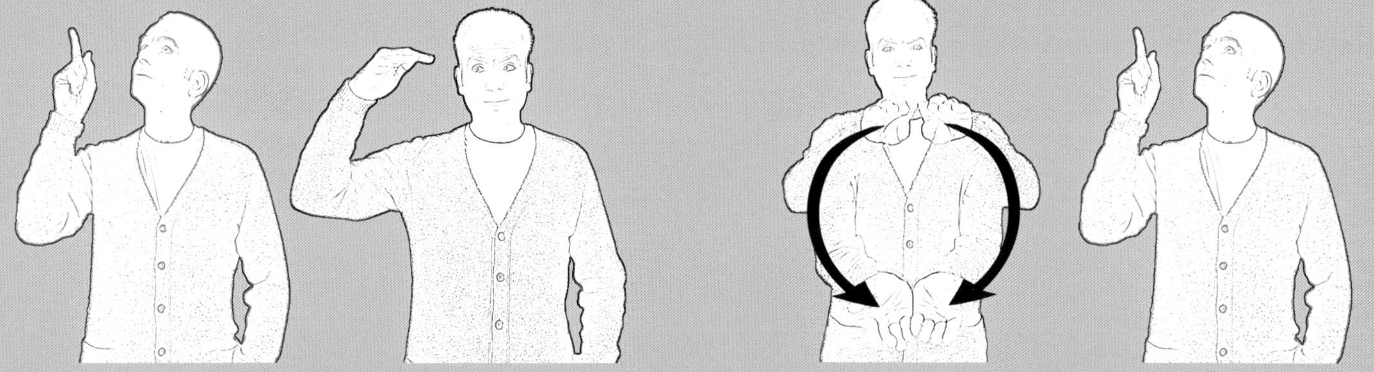

Up above *the* world *so* high

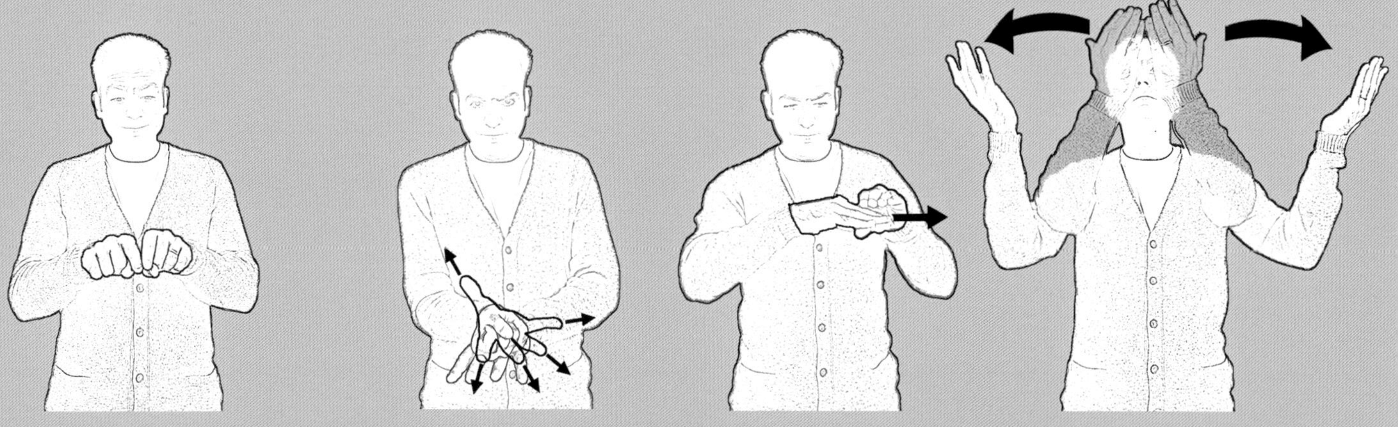

Like *a* diamond in *the* sky

HELLO
GOODBYE
EVERYONE
NICE to
SEE
YOU
HERE
Two taps of M
MUMMY
Two taps of F
DADDY
Mummy or Daddy
GRAND
FAMILY
BROTHER
SISTER
Tap nose twice
BOY
GIRL
Stroke lip twice

PLEASE
THANK YOU
YES
NO
GOOD
GREAT
BEST
MORNING
DAY
NIGHT
MAN
WOMAN
YOU
ME

BIRD FISH TURTLE

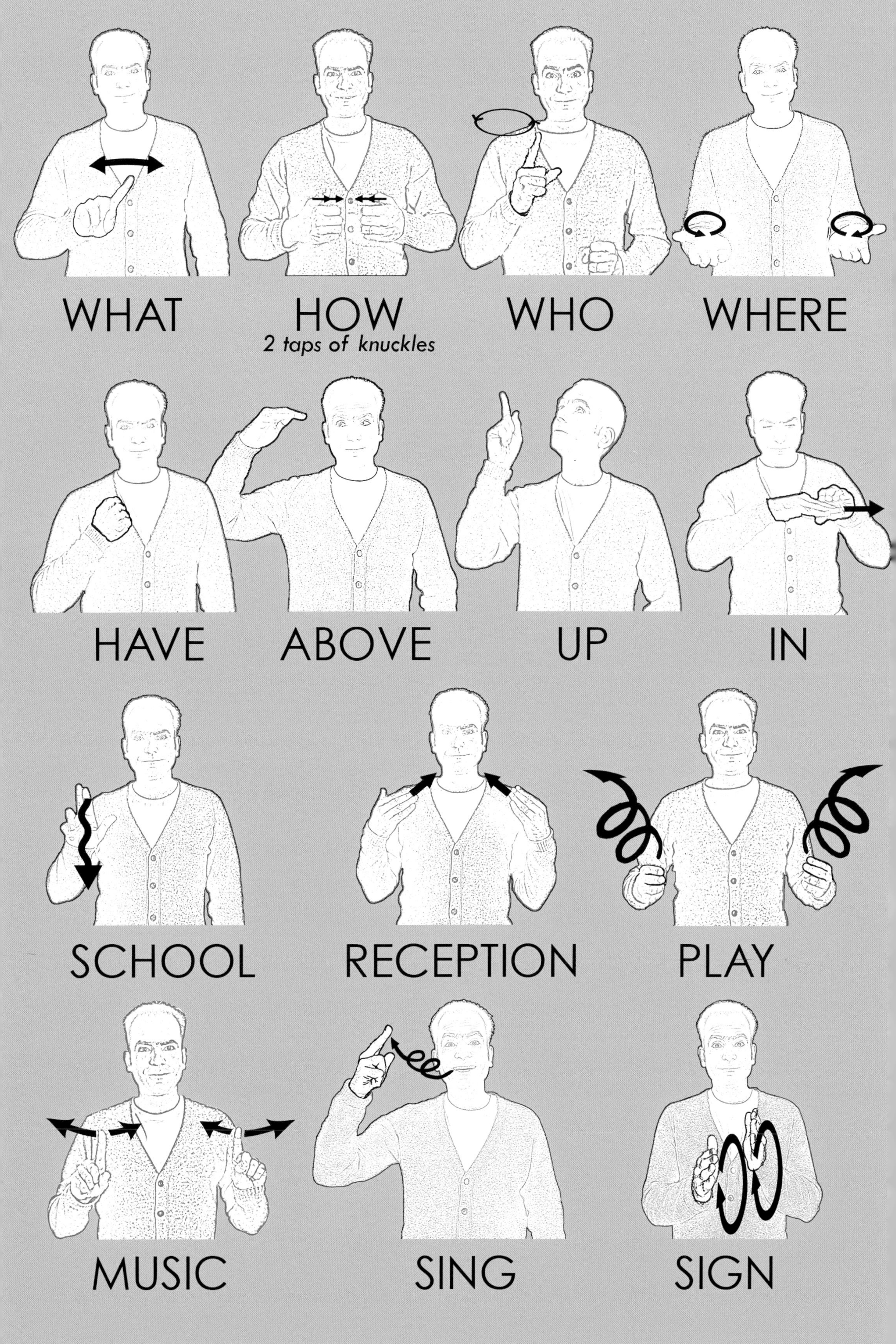
WHAT
HOW
2 taps of knuckles
WHO
WHERE
HAVE
ABOVE
UP
IN
SCHOOL
RECEPTION
PLAY
MUSIC
SING
SIGN

MOON
SUN
STAR
SKY
RAIN
RAINBOW
SNOW
COLD
SOAP
BATH
BED
HALLOWEEN
PUMPKIN
FIREWORKS

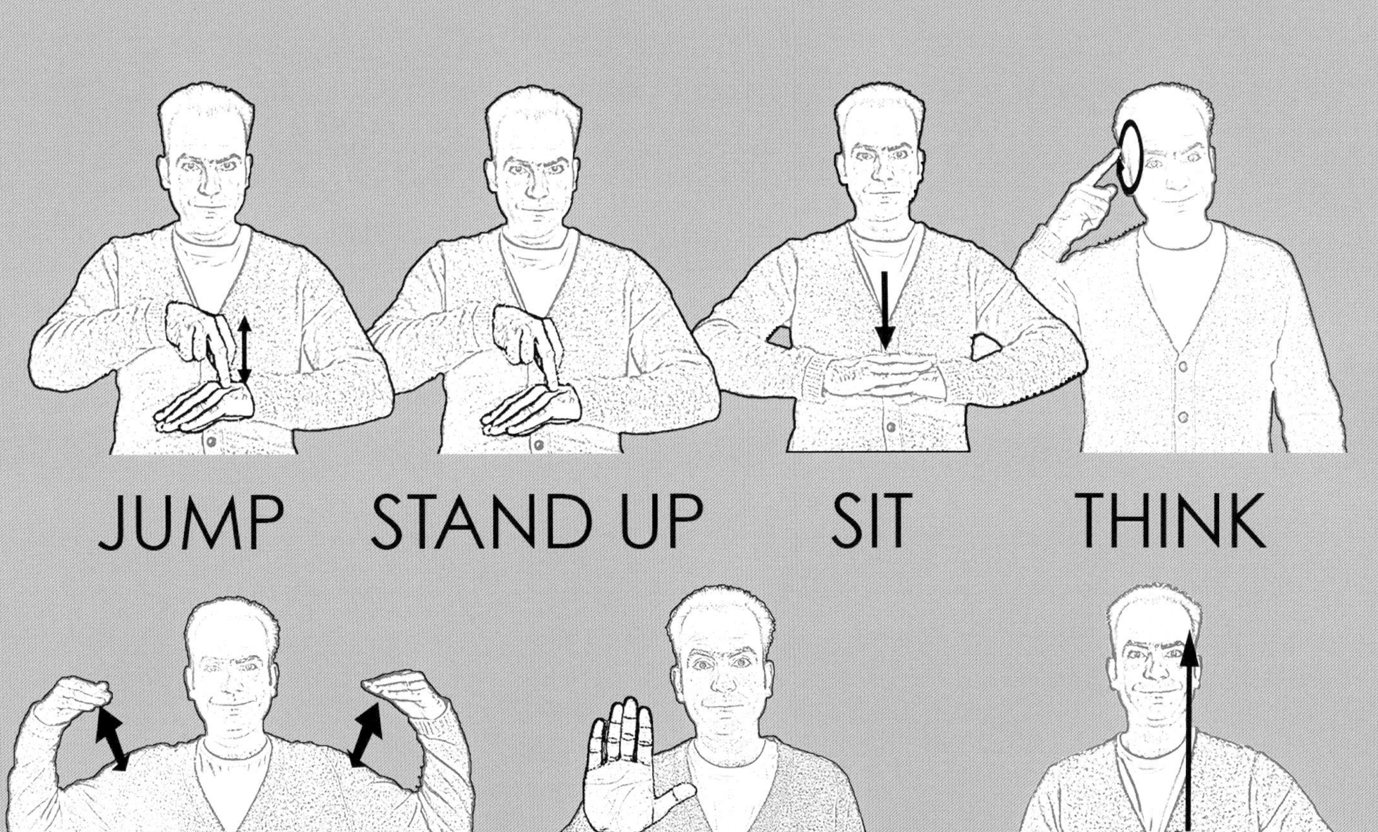
JUMP
STAND UP
SIT
THINK

EXERCISE
STOP
ROCKET
CAR
AEROPLANE
TRAIN
HELICOPTER

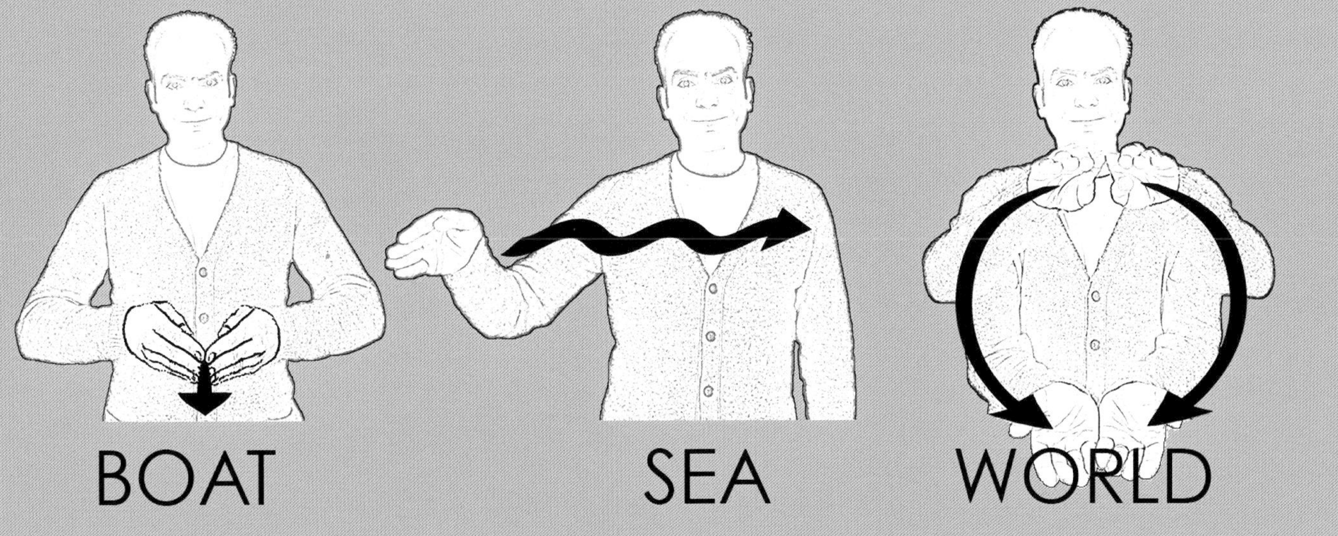
BOAT
SEA
WORLD

SETTING UP FOR MUSIC

Music is a great group activity. You don't need to have a lot of people for the communal energy to work its magic. These guidelines of how to set up for a music session will work well at home with friends and family or in a nursery/school setting.

For me, the best way to start a music session is with everyone sitting on the floor. Coats off. Shoes off. On the floor. In a circle. The area should be carpeted or covered in mats, so that everyone is comfortable.

Set up a circle of instruments, placing them where you want people to sit. I always like giving the children a name sticker, they're useful and fun. Use as wide a variety of instruments and sound toys as possible. Shakers, drums, sticks, bells, glockenspiels and xylophones, triangles, scrapers, whistles, gathering drums, the list is endless. I love making instruments from everyday and recycled objects. Shakers from bottles and beans, drums from empty tins and tubs, rain-sticks from cardboard tubes and rice, scrapers from soap dishes, guitars, kazoos, chicken squeakers. Your imagination is the only limit.

It's good for the children to have something to hold in their hand, be it a beater, stick or small shaker. This can be used in all the games to beat rhythms and patterns on the floor, drums or other instruments.

Keep the sessions exciting and engaging, using lots of movement and actions. Using makaton signs as the actions in some of the songs, introduces a new way of communicating and guarantees that we all use the same actions. Props like colourful play parachutes, hand puppets, peek-a-boo cloths and song props help to keep things exciting and are a great focal point.

It is essential to be sensitive to the children's collective mood, so having session plans is great, but you must be ready to adapt them.

Introduce and discover new styles and genres of music for listening and playing. You will soon discover which your children prefer from their response. Some styles that I have found work particularly well include Ska, Skiffle, House, Disco, Northern Soul, Funk, Cumbia and Samba. But use the music you enjoy, and hopefully the kids will too!

Db C# Eb D# Gb F# Ab G# Bb A# Db C# Eb D# Gb F# Ab G# Bb A# Db C# Eb D#

C D E F G A B C D E F G A B C D E

I've never been taught the guitar, but it is fairly easy to master a few chords.
Nearly all of the songs in this book can be played with these 2 sets of chords.
The lines represent the strings and the dots are where your fingers go.
O means play the open string. X means don't play the string.

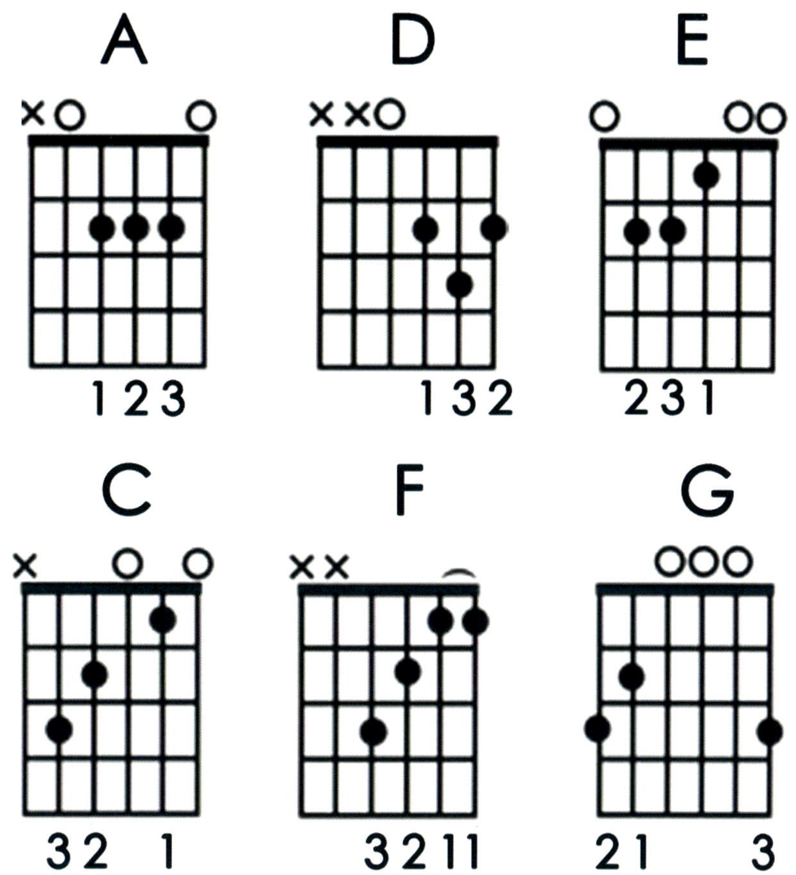

I LIKE SINGING SONGS – CD TRACKS

1 SHAKE 'EM UP HIGH
2 SHAKE AND STOP
3 A FRIEND I KNOW
4 HELLO
5 I AM GREAT
6 WHO I AM
7 WHO LIVES IN THE JUNGLE?
8 LITTLE GREEN FROG
9 MR FROG
10 KING OF KINGS
11 GONNA DO OUR EXERCISE
12 WAKE UP, WAKE UP
13 JUMPING ALL DAY LONG
14 I LIKE SINGING SONGS
15 I'M A FREEBIRD
16 IF I WAS A...
17 I SEE A BOAT
18 MAMA PAQUITA
19 HEAR THE TRAIN
20 THE WHEELS ON THE BUS
21 STEAM TRAIN
22 YOU ARE THE SEASONS
23 JAMBO BWANA
24 UP ABOVE MY HEAD
25 BAA BAA/TWINKLE TWINKLE/ABC
26 TWINKLE TWINKLE/ABC
27 OLD MACDONALD
28 ROW ROW ROW YOUR BOAT
29 LEMONADE
30 I LIKE BANANAS
31 HERE'S MY RHYTHM
32 FLEA, FLY, MOSQUITO
33 BOOM CHICKA BOOM
34 PEEK A BOO
35 THREE BIG BALLOONS
36 POPCORN
37 TINY TIM
38 OPEN SHUT THEM

CORIN–THE MUSIC MAN–PRESENTS–I LIKE SINGING SONGS
First published - 2016 by Learning Curve Music
This edition published by Learning Curve Music 2016
LEARNING CURVE MUSIC PUBLISHING
HASTINGS
U.K
www.ilikesingingsongs.com
For information about special discounts for bulk purchases,
workshops, teacher packs and more visit
www.ilikesingingsongs.com

Editoriol consultant Sam Sweeney
Design consultant Michael Smee
Proof reading Deborah Stuart and Mum and Dad
ISBN 978-0-9956050-0-8

A CIP catalogue for this book is available from
the British Library.

Printed by KNOCKOUT PRINT, KENT, UK